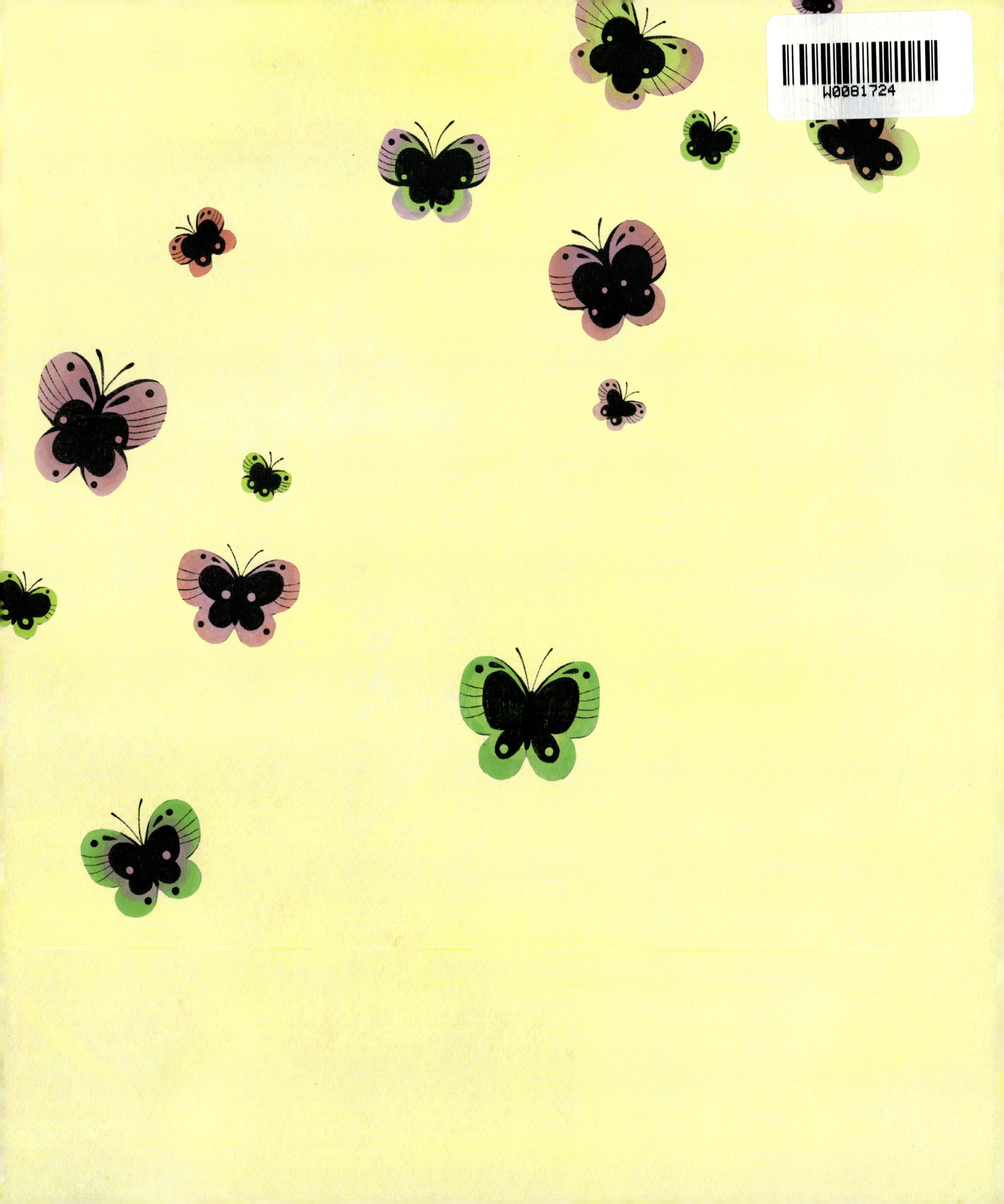

For poets and readers everywhere, especially to the

anthologists who first recognized our poems: Georgia Heard,

the late Lee Bennett Hopkins, the late Paul B. Janeczko,

J. Patrick Lewis, Sylvia Vardell, and Janet Wong

And to the editor who joyfully embraced this work:

Liz Bicknell

IL & CW

To my dad, Jose, and my brother, Gabe

OS

Compilation copyright © 2025 by Irene Latham and Charles Waters
Illustrations copyright © 2025 by Olivia Sua
Copyright acknowledgments appear on pages 52–53.

First edition 2025

Library of Congress Control Number: 2024944213
ISBN 978-1-5362-1979-1

24 25 26 27 28 29 APS 10 9 8 7 6 5 4 3 2 1

Printed in Humen, Dongguan, China

This book was typeset in Cabin.
The illustrations were done in mixed media.

Candlewick Press
99 Dover Street
Somerville, Massachusetts 02144

www.candlewick.com

EU Authorized Representative: HackettFlynn Ltd.,
36 Cloch Choirneal, Balrothery, Co. Dublin, K32 C942, Ireland.
EU@walkerpublishinggroup.com

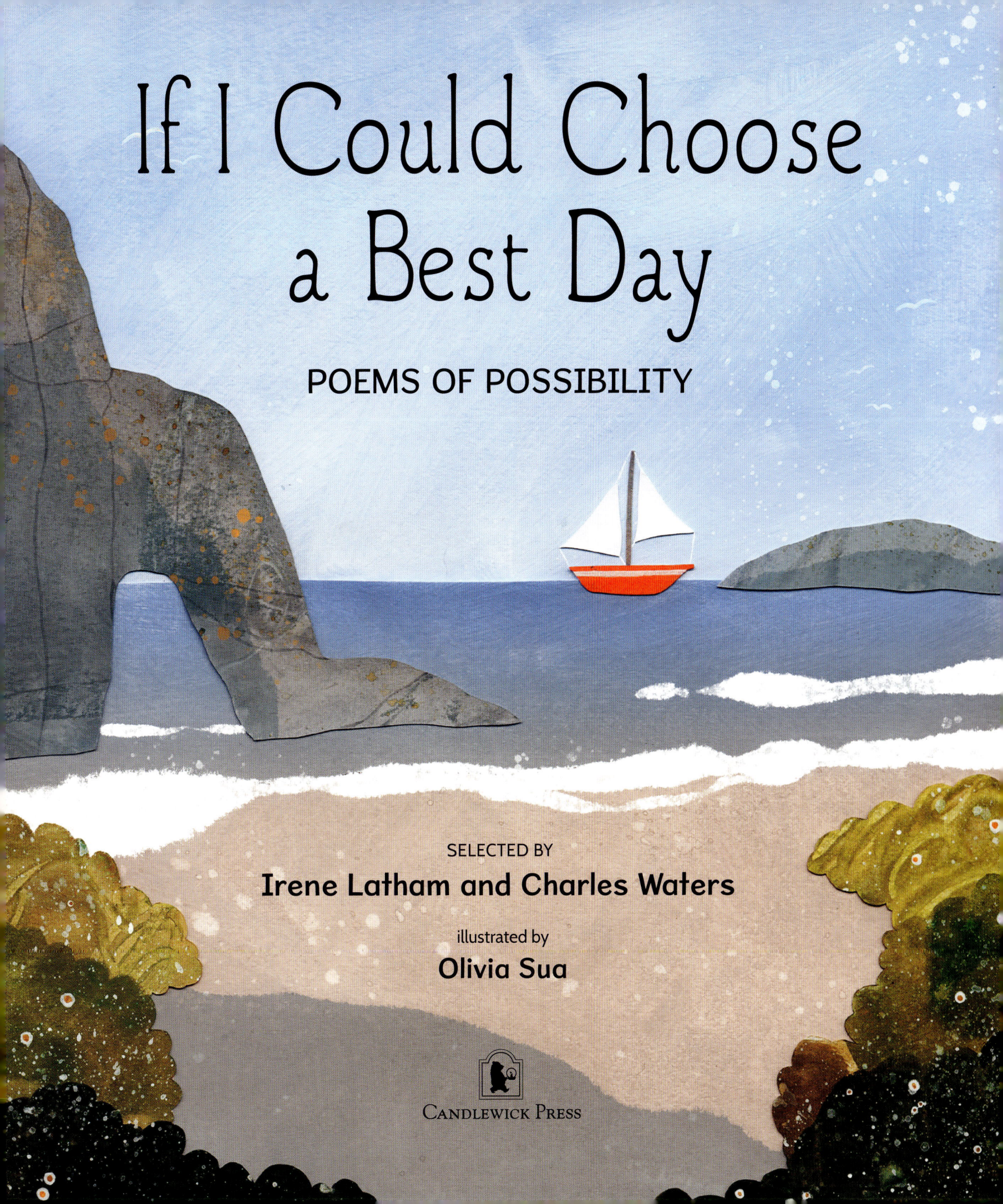

If I Could Choose a Best Day

POEMS OF POSSIBILITY

SELECTED BY

Irene Latham and Charles Waters

illustrated by

Olivia Sua

CANDLEWICK PRESS

CONTENTS

Welcome

by Irene Latham and Charles Waters

If you're reading this,

it's time to unlock

the door to Possibility.

Trust yourself—

        turn the key.

EVERYDAY MAGIC

If You Have a Pencil

by Eric Ode

If you have a pencil,
you might make a poem.
If you have a tire,
you might make a swing.
You might make a tower
of buckets and boxes.
You might make a kite
out of paper and string.

You might make a story
of dreams and adventure,
a dash of imagine,
a cup of pretend.
If you have a pencil,
you might make a poem.
If you have a smile,
you just might make a friend.

If Ever You Build a Tree House

by Rebecca Kai Dotlich

If ever you build a tree house
in a city or a town
make sure it has the kind of steps
that go both up and down.

And then whatever else you do
make sure it has a door
for going in and out of it
both after and before.

Then find a hidden spot for dreams
that ever and ever might be
both then and now and now and then
where you can be you
            in a house in a tree.

Finch, Robin, Jay

by Amy Ludwig VanDerwater

If you learn the name of just one bird
one bird that lives not far from you

if you learn the patterns on its wings
recognize which song it sings

then every time you see this bird
you will feel a friend is near—

a nesting friend
a flying friend.

Your heart will grin.
Your mind will clear.

You will feel big and small at once
if you learn the name of just one bird.

If You Catch a Firefly

by Lilian Moore

If you catch a firefly
    and keep it in a jar
You may find that
    you have lost
A tiny star.

If you let it go then,
    back into the night,
You may see it
    once again
Star bright.

The Rock

by Sarah Grace Tuttle

If you look closer
the rock has veins that glimmer

if you look closer
the glimmer ripples like water

if you look closer
in the ripples are

          mermaids.

If a Bad Dream Comes

by Siv Cedering

If a bad dream comes
and scares me awake,
I pull the covers over my head
and hide
inside
the small warm room
of my bed.

My blanket is a ceiling.
My mattress is a floor.
The covers tucked tight
are the corners of the walls.
And my pillow is a door
that I can lock
against
the night.

It's dark in this room,
and it almost feels safe,
but if someone should come
to see if I'm awake,
if someone should ask
"Who is hiding there?"
I'd say:
"It's me—and I'm scared."

Opening Windows
by Teresa Owens Smith

If you cannot sleep, open the windows.
Search the dark sea of the night sky.
Your dreams are hiding there.
You cannot keep them quiet and shy.

Grab the stars and let moonlight dance inside you.

THE POWER OF YOU

What Kind of Word Is *If*?

by Georgia Heard

If is a wise word,
a wishing word,
   a winged word
   that flies in the blue
   sky of hope,
a longing word,
a listening word,
   a word to hold
   gently in the palm
   of your hands,
a borderless word,
a believing word,
a *don't give up* word,
a *pick yourself up* word,
a beginning word,
a belonging word,
     an *I can* word,
     an *I am* word.

If I Imagine Sunlight Made Me

by Lacresha Berry

If I imagine

sunlight made me

my soul soars

like a blackbird

chirping in celebration

of my midnight wings

without anyone

telling me

I am too dark

to be related

to the sun.

Time

by Rebekah Lowell

If you give a tadpole time,
it will change into a frog.

If you give an egg time,
it will hatch into a bird.

If you give a seed time,
it will bloom into a flower.

If you give a caterpillar time,
it will morph into a butterfly.

If you give an acorn time,
it will grow into an oak.

If you give yourself time,
just think what you will do.

"If I can stop one Heart from breaking"

by Emily Dickinson

If I can stop one Heart from breaking

I shall not live in vain

If I can ease one Life the Aching

Or cool one Pain

Or help one fainting Robin

Unto his Nest again

I shall not live in Vain.

"If this wind persists"

by Sydell Rosenberg

If this wind persists

I'll be blown into a shape—

like a bonsai tree!

If a Snowstorm Comes to Town

by Janice Scully

If a snowstorm comes to town,
I'll watch the snowflakes falling down,
watch them swirling to the ground
sparkling, spinning round and round.
Never will they make a sound
just keep falling
down
    down
        down.

I love to watch the snowflakes fall—
no one rushes snow at all!
Out my window, wandering free,
snow is how I like to be.

If I Were a Bookworm

by Guadalupe García McCall

If I were a bookworm
I'd feast on millions of words.
I'd wrap them in masa,
cook them on firewood,
and top them with salsa.

I'd chew cold words too,
words so chilled and frosty
my fingers would tingle
as I patted them down
with *ajo* and *comino*!

I'd munch on sweet words
because they make me smile.
Words dripping with icing
and stuffed with *fruta*
son deliciosas—very enticing!

I'd make short work
of *palabras malas*—
words vile and malicious.
I'd cut, stir fry, and sauté
them, until they were tender—
so nice and nutritious.

If I were a bookworm
I'd tear through so many words
that my *dientes* would hurt—
but my heart would dance
and my soul would feel good.

KINFOLK AND COMPANIONS

If, Then

by Jolene Gutiérrez

If you, then me.
If two, then three.

If look, then see.
If us, then we.

If stars, then sun.
If day, then fun.

If catch, then fall.
If love, then all.

If speak, then hear.
If far, then near.

If We Were Rich

by Janet Wong

"If I was rich,
I would buy Mommy a new coat."
That's what my brother says.

Mommy says
she's not going anywhere special.
She doesn't want a new coat.

"If I was rich,
I would buy Mommy a new house."
That's what I say.

Mommy says
she loves our neighbors.
She doesn't want a new house.

"What can we buy you, then?" we ask.
"Nothing," she says, and tells us
to rub her tired feet.

We cuddle under a quilt
on our comfy old couch.
It's okay that we're not rich.

Puddle

by Bob Raczka

If this puddle could
Talk, I think it would tell me
To splash my sister.

30

Scattered

by Nancy Tupper Ling

If I scatter words
like paper puddles
across our kitchen floor,
I find *morning*
next to *moonlight*,
龙 (*dragon*)
beside 米 (*rice*).
If I fling them overhead,
they fall, colorful
stepping stones,
blending Mama's
and Baba's worlds
into a path
here at my feet.

Blue Bike

by Gabi Snyder

If I could pedal my blue bike
back through time, I'd pedal
back to Grandma's house
to sit next to her on the sun-flowered
couch. We'd drink lemonade
with the fan blowing back and forth
to cool our faces, talking about her childhood—
the tornado that knocked their gas station flat,
the lake she swam across, and the tree she climbed
out the attic window down to her blue bike,
ready for adventure.

If I Could Choose a Best Day

by Lisa Rogers

If I could choose a best day
it would be sunny
it would be summer

and I would be with you,

eating blueberries
mouth-puckering and sweet

searching for clover
to braid into crowns

tracking ants
on their journeys to somewhere
and back

staying so still
dragonflies could rest—
ever so lightly—
on our fingertips

stretching in skin-prickling grass
eyes closed

breathing

the humming world
around us.

No In-Between

by Anna Grossnickle Hines

If one is right
the other wrong
how can we ever
get along?

If We Listen

by Joseph Bruchac

If we listen long enough
might we hear what the birds
are telling us?

Our old people did—
they knew those songs
to greet the coming of the sun
were messages
to understand:

Look to the light.
You are not alone.

Listen to the birds,
to the bright life
all around,
and you may find
your own hymn.

ANYTHING IS POSSIBLE

Journey

by Nikki Grimes

If I shatter the wall
between dream and
what might be,
I could say "kite"
and the wind of my words
would rocket me into the air
where I could soar,
skip round the sun,
take a leisurely tour
of cumulus clouds,
or fly in formation
with geese gathered for
their annual commute
to warmer climes.
No, I'm not
a feathered creature,
but this flight of mind
is real—
if I say so.

If You Catch a Magic Fish

by Sylvia Liu

If you catch a magic fish
that grants you but a single wish,
will you ask for coins and gold,
to live forever, not grow old?
Will you seek to end all war,
to never have another chore?

I'd wonder what the fish would say.
Would it rather swim away
and live a life that's wild and free
instead of toil for you or me?

If you catch a magic fish,
why not ask what *it* would wish?

A World Without Hate

by Vikram Madan

If frogs grew on trees . . .
If rainbows laid eggs . . .
If dogs flew like bees . . .
If houses had legs . . .

If shoes liked to sing . . .
If fish played trombones . . .
If each year, in spring,
it rained ice cream cones . . .

If all this was true . . .
If we met face to face . . .
I would surely like you—
    and I'm sure you'd like me—
for a world without hate
is a magical place.

Nobody Remembers

by Laura Purdie Salas

If everybody was healthy,
the hospital would empty out.

All around,
kids would hit pop flies,
granddads would tend roses,
grown-ups would push strollers,
ice cream trucks would sing down streets,
beagles would ask for belly rubs,
and teachers would share stories,
until, finally,

one day,

the hospital would be
just a dusty shadow,
and nobody would remember
what was ever there.

A Glimmer of Peace

by Robyn Hood Black

If you spin
your silky dreams,
then
 wait
  breathe—
let peace unfurl
moonshimmer wings.

48

One Stitch

by Renée M. LaTulippe

If each kind deed could be

a square of cloth,

and each kind word

a stitch,

and if each day we shared

another square,

another stitch,

soon we'd have a quilt of kindness

big enough to blanket

our   whole   patchwork   world.

The Gift of *If*

by JaNay Brown-Wood

If is a gift for adventure
If is a "huh?" to explore
If is a gripping story
egging you on—don't stop, read more!

If is an unanswered question
If is a boredom cure
If is an arching rainbow—
no one knows where it ends for sure.

If is a lost, buried treasure
If is a padlocked door
If is the thought "what's out there?"
without a clue of what's in store.

And *if* means there is no limit
If means forget before
If means all is possible
Because *if* means the world is yours!

A Note from Irene Latham and Charles Waters

Every child wonders. Every child has spent minutes, days, years in the land of "if." As two people who have been known to stare out of windows, just wondering, we know firsthand how it's exactly this kind of *if*-ing that gives our lives meaning, value, and excitement and provides a necessary balm in the midst of chaos. In fact, it's between the letters *i* and *f* that dreams are born and achieved. Imagination is the very thing that fuels technology and progress. And imagination is where we'll find the answers to how to make the world a better place.

We're committed to bringing the best poems to young people. With that in mind, we created an open call for poetic submissions through social media. We offered a weeklong submission window and asked people to share the opportunity far and wide. This allowed everyone an equal chance to have their work considered for inclusion. We received nearly four hundred poems from around the world. Critique groups sent us poems, unpublished writers sent out their work for the first time, and award-winning writers emailed us poems as well. The process of reading each one was humbling and exhilarating. We're so grateful to each person for taking a leap in the name of poetry and allowing us to read their work.

Selecting the poems that were the best fit for this anthology was quite a challenge, as we found something to love in nearly all the submissions. Alas, a book can only hold so many poems! Our goal was to give each poem the same respect and care it was given when the poet crafted the poem in the first place.

We also spent many a day and night searching existing collections in libraries, bookstores, and our own bookshelves for previously published poems in order to make this the most comprehensive and representative collection possible within our criteria. Special shout-out to the now-defunct Bank Street Bookstore in NYC—which closed in 2020 after fifty years—for helping us find some of the poems in this book that had already been published.

As always, we're so grateful to our literary agent, Rosemary Stimola, and all the talented, kind humans at Stimola Literary Studio for their continued support.

Finally, *if* Liz Bicknell and Candlewick Press hadn't taken a chance on this book by two relatively new anthologists, these poetic pages wouldn't be in your hands right now. Thank you, Liz and Candlewick! Additional thanks to Carter Hasegawa for his assistance during the editorial process.

Wishing you strength and joy always,

Irene & Charles